Kids Talk Hair

An Instruction Book for Grown-Ups & Kids

Al Eta

MAI

Nozani Rogers

Audrey Hailes

Klaiama

Vandruang Ferrell

Patrice Rodgers

Anne Phillips

Kamila Mack

Madaya

This Book Belongs To:

_____

_____

_____

Amber Ferrell

Michael Lester

Mark Johnson

Jordanna Bradley

Dan

Kierro

Simone Stroman

Raven Jeffers

Afra Abdullah

Nia Pride

AAVFM

Kids Talk Hair

An Instruction Book for Grown-Ups & Kids

Pamela Ferrell

Foreword by Marian Wright-Edelman

Edited by Sabrina Holcomb

Cornrows & Co. Publishing
Washington, DC

KIDS TALK HAIR: An Instruction Book for Grown-Ups & Kids
by Pamela Ferrell
Published by Cornrows & Co.
5401 14th Street NW ▪ Washington, DC 20011

Printed in Hong Kong, 10 9 8 7 6 5 4 3 2
Library of Congress Catalog Card Number: 99-072491
Cataloging In Publication
ISBN: 0-939183-03-X

Editor ..... Sabrina Holcomb
Book Design ..... Pamela Ferrell
Photography ..... Andre Richardson, Sonnie Mason

Visit www.cornrowsandco.com

Table of Contents

Acknowledgments

A million hugs and kisses to all my children in the book. You all were perfect models during the shampoo day and especially at the photo session. No make-up and no coaching -- I think ya'll must of done some modeling in a previous life.

Hip hip hurrah to the parents who trusted me with their precious ones. Without you the little ones could not have arrived on time. And with your blessing, you help made it happen. My most sincere thank you for allowing me the pleasure of having your child in the book.

Mom & Dad, thanks for letting me do my own hair at a very young age. Not once did you frown on my creative hair styles. I look back at my kid pictures and wonder how you let me go out the house looking like that. You must have known that with practice, one day I'd be able to create some great hair styles.

Andre Richardson, the computer guru — thanks for your graphic and design support. Tia, Juan, Corene, Sharon, Roberta, Shuletta, Felicita, Sade, Tamara, Tonya, Victoria and Barbara, it takes a village (staff) to keep a group of kids busy. I am grateful that you all were my eyes, ears, and hands (since I had tendonitis in my wrist) for getting the kids ready for the camera. Thanks for your great styles and helping hands.

Taalib-Din, my husband, as always you keep the nuts and bolts of the business in order, which allows me to freely create and not sweat the big stuff.

Phyllis Brown, you named the book *Kids Talk Hair*. Thanks, homegirl (for real).

Pamela Ferrell

Note to grown-ups

Kids have a good sense of style and will tell grown-ups what they like and dislike if they feel it's okay to express themselves. And freedom of expression helps build their self-confidence.

I learned this when I planned the kids' photo shoot. I usually plan hair styles in advance. Well, on this occasion most of the kids did not want the styles that I had planned for them. Mark (wearing freedom hair on page 41) decided he did not want his hair braided after we shampooed and dried his Afro bush. Little princess Afra (page 37) repeatedly suggested that I put a decorative comb on her little ponytail, even after I explained the comb was for holding a big ponytail. Well, to my surprise the comb made a beautiful crown for her ponytail. So, I listened to their ideas. Many of the hair styles in the book, they suggested to me as I was actually doing their hair or just before camera time.

God knows, the lesson I learned is to let kids express their idea of style and let them help choose the hair styles they will wear. It's no question that when "kids talk hair," we just have to listen.

Marian Wright Edelman
President, The Children's Defense Fund

Foreword by Marian Wright-Edelman

Life has just gotten a little easier for parents. With this book, help is on the way for parents who have the responsibility of doing hair. I have raised three boys, which made my hair care responsibilities as easy as going to the barber. But I could have used Pam Ferrell's *Kids Talk Hair* when I was growing up.

As the president and founder of the Children's Defense Fund, I am an advocate for the children of America who cannot vote, lobby or speak for themselves. Our mission is to Leave No Child Behind and to ensure every child has a Healthy Start, Head Start, Fair Start, and Moral Start in life. With the help of caring families and communities we can ensure that every child has a successful passage to adulthood.

In my work and in my life, I have discovered that it is the little things, like spending quality time with children, listening to them, making them feel good about themselves and hopeful about their future, that strengthens families. Parents will welcome this practical book to make daily responsibilities like hair care an easy task and a time for bonding with their children.

On my visits to the Cornrows & Co. Salon, I can remember seeing little girls as young as three years old sitting up having their hair braided, as if they had been doing this for many years. I watched with joy when I saw their faces blossom with pride and appreciation when they walked to the big mirror to look at their newly done hair. Those are special, uplifting moments for children, moments to be shared with parents either at home or at the salon.

In a time when both parents often must work to make ends meet, and many women face raising their children alone, working mothers must stretch each hour to its maximum. A book like this is a wonderful tool for doing something that can be as fun for you and your child as it is necessary.

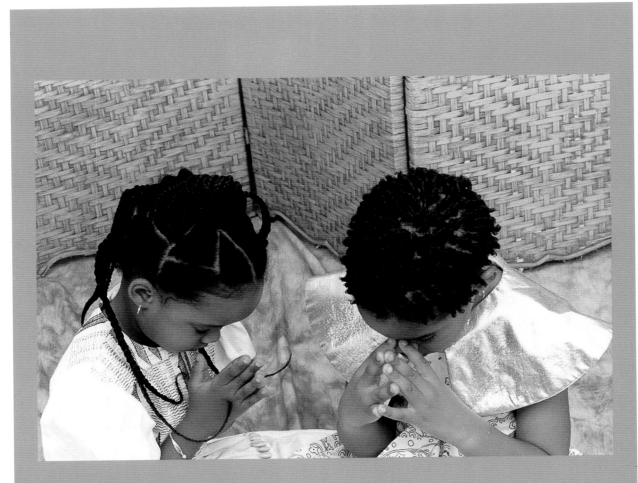

We have hair like Angels.
Thank you, dear God.

The Beginning

When kids come into your life, there is one very important thing that is missing —instructions. Kids don't come with instructions when they are born. Some things you just know, like giving love, sweet kisses, big hugs and feeding them. But we learn about hair care the hard way — through sheer necessity and the mere fact that their hair will need to be combed at some point in their lives! Hair care the hard way has left some tearful and unpleasant hair experiences. And it doesn't help when family, friends and perfect strangers all have hair care advice you really don't need.

I imagine that all this trial and error stuff could be avoided if there were simple, user-friendly hair care instructions for grown-ups. Instructions that explain: how kids' hair grows; how to shampoo or get gum out of hair; how to deal with head lice, ringworm and comb-out disasters and, mostly, how to make pretty hair styles.

So, I prayed for this book and the "Hair Angel" answered. The Hair Angel arrived just in time to share some earthly tips on just what to do to make hair care a terrific and exciting event for grown-ups and kids.

Did you know that kids have hair like Angels? Yes they do. It's hair that has God's blessings. So, with the help of the Hair Angel, we have put together an instruction book for grown-ups *and* kids to use. It's easy to read and simple to follow. Many of the left-hand pages are for young kids to read, and the right-hand pages are for grown-ups and big kids.

I've given my input, kids have talked hair to me and I've gotten some Angel tips for heavenly hair. So, open your mind and get ready to explore some good-spirited ideas for kids' healthy hair care.

My newborn hair is five weeks old. How old is your hair?

NEWBORN HAIR

Infant to three years old

Babies don't come home from the hospital with baby-care instructions. So what about infant hair care? You surely don't want to treat our delicate new hair like you would yours. Newborn hair is special. Some babies are born bald, while others have so much hair you can't see the scalp. Just keep in mind that the scalp is delicate and the hair follicles are still developing. Here are three things to do for newborn hair.

1 First, protect my head and scalp from the elements, things like hot sun, wind, rain and cold weather. You'll notice a pulsating soft spot at the top center of my head. It's called the fontanel. My skull is growing and eventually it will close in so that the soft spot disappears. For hot weather use a sheer cotton covering, and for cold weather use a medium-weight, natural cotton or wool fabric to keep my head comfortably warm.

Grown-ups, be smart about the hats and headbands you put on our heads. Comfort is more important than what's cute. Babies are not dolls, so think about what is going to cause us discomfort. Head gear may be cute but you don't know if it's irritating, too tight and pulling on our newborn hairs.

When kids are born our hair is soft, shiny, straight or curly. Sometimes we don't have any hair, but it will grow soon. Be very careful with our heads. And be very gentle when you touch our hair, because it's brand new.

Love us, hug us, and teach us to love ourselves. We already know this when we are born. But with your

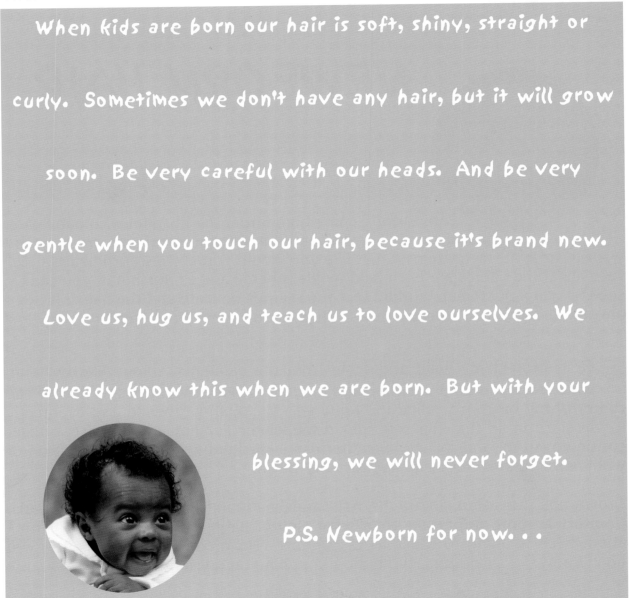

blessing, we will never forget.

P.S. Newborn for now. . .

2 Second, clean my scalp when you bathe me. Simply, wash my hair by gently rubbing it with a washcloth. Use a mild natural liquid soap that does not leave a film. Newborn hair is soft enough to lay in place by wiping it with a washcloth. No need for conditioners. A light natural oil (Cornrows & Co. Jasmine spray oil) is perfect for rubbing on my head and moisturizing my skin. Avoid synthetic, greasy petroleum or mineral oil products.

3 Third, expect my newborn hair to change during the first two years of my life. Usually my hair is very soft. Sometimes it's stick straight or sometimes it's curly at birth. By the time I come home from the hospital, my hair will start to wave and form a curl. After about three months, it will start to curl and frizz. My hair texture is magical, so enjoy the changes and don't try to make it what it's not going to be. Don't try to keep it straight when its nature is to curl. Celebrate my hair as it takes on its own texture.

After about six months you may notice my hair thinning in the areas I lay on the most (back and sides). Don't worry, my hair will grow back once the hair follicle matures and I can roll over and sleep in different positions.

See my hair on page 65

If your baby's hair is thick and long enough to braid, *do not braid the hair tight*. This can cause permanent hair loss. Braid the hair softly, in simple styles, and expect to re-braid it every day. Also, do not put barrettes on the back and sides of your baby's head. They are uncomfortable to lay on and can pull the hair out.

Have you noticed patches of dandruff on your baby's head? Or a crusty white or yellowish scaly plaque that forms a cap on the scalp? This is cradle cap (*crusta lactea*). It's a common scalp condition found in young babies. Cradle cap goes away after the first year, but it can mean that your child may be predisposed to eczema.

A biotin deficiency may be responsible for cradle cap. Biotin is one of the B vitamins that helps to improve the production of scalp oils and normal intestinal flora. To heal cradle cap, treat the condition both topically and nutritionally with biotin-rich foods. Foods that contain biotin include brewer's yeast, cauliflower, soybeans, egg yolks, peanuts, oatmeal, black-eyed peas, whole wheat, brown rice germ and rice bran. A mother who is breast-feeding can take biotin herself or give it to her baby. You can purchase a biotin supplement for infants at health-food stores or check with your doctor of naturopathy.

To treat cradle cap topically, rub one of the following on your baby's scalp. Try all of them to see which one gives you the best results:

- Vitamin E and Almond oils with crushed Vitamin B6 tablets.

- Poultice made from the Figwort herb *(Scrophularia Nodose)*. (A poultice is made from a mixture of the herbs with warm water, spread on a cloth.)

- Vitamin E oil

1. Rub one of these preparations on the dry areas in the morning, thirty minutes before bathing your baby, then wash it off. Apply again in the afternoon, where needed.

2. In a severe case of cradle cap, rub Vitamin E oil on the scalp after your baby's evening bath and leave on overnight.

Kids' hair grows on its own, like beautiful flowers, big, small, short and tall.

Kids' Hair Grows on its Own

From the time we are conceived, our bodies have genetic instructions that program our hair color, length and texture. Grown-ups, you cannot change this and you certainly don't have any control over it after we are born.

So, don't worry about how fast our hair grows. Some kids are born bald and don't grow a full head of hair until three years old, like Afyiah on the opposite page. Other kids are born with a head full of hair, and it will come out then grow back in. Our little bodies are developing, and so are the hair follicles. It can take up to three years or more for a kid's hair to grow into its full length and strength.

Be patient and grateful for our blessed hair. Don't do any crazy things to make it grow faster than it naturally will. God knows exactly how fast our hair should grow, so trust in time that we will grow plenty of hair.

- Don't pull our braids tight in order to make our hair grow fast.

- Don't straighten our hair to make it look long.

- Don't use "hair-grow grease" on our scalps.

- Don't hang us upside down.

- And please, no wigs.

- Just love our hair the way it is, thank you very much!

God likes colors and so do I.

Kids' Hair Colors

I think God likes colors and so do I. The world is not made in black and white. There are many colors of flowers, fruits, trees, animals, people and hair.

It does not matter what color hair we are born with because all hair is beautiful. Can you name the many colors of hair?

- Raven has Red hair with gold and orange hair mixed in. When the light shines on her hair, it looks like the autumn leaves.

- Patrice has Black shiny hair. Yummy, it looks like delicious licorice candy.

- Xenia has Brown hair. It makes me think of chocolate, chocolate cookies.

- Ray-Ray has Tan hair. It's a pretty light-brown color with gold hair mixed in. Her hair is brown like baked bread crust.

- Wendy has Gold hair. Some people say it's blonde, but I think it's Gold.

- Auntie has Grey hair. Kind of like a squirrel's hair. I think it's mixed-up black and white.

Nana has Silver and White hair. It sparkles in the sun and is soft like cotton candy.

My hair is Red. What color is your hair?

▪ Green, blue or purple hair? I remember my friend's sister went to the hair salon, and she came back with purple hair. I don't know what happened because in the morning her hair was brown. I'm not gonna change my hair color because I like it and God likes it too.

Q.) Can you name these different hair colors?

Q.) Do you know how hair gets its natural color?

Hair has three layers. The first layer is outside. It 's the clear protector, kind of like your fingernail. The second layer has many grains that give hair its color, like grains of salt make white and grains of pepper make black. The third layer is inside. It gives hair its strength. If you try to change the color of our hair, you may hurt one of the layers. So let's keep kids' hair color just the way God made it.

Kids' hair care is different from grown-ups.
When we go to play, our hair comes with us.

All About Kids' Hair

and what to do to take care of it . . .

Our hair is different from yours.
It's dirtier because we play. It doesn't stay neat long.
And we have our own styles.

Rumble in the dirt•••

That's why the ends of our hair are very dirty. Don't be alarmed by the dirty, muddy lather when you shampoo our hair. It's just that kids' hair goes where no hair has gone before. Grown-ups just don't know all the places our hair may visit. Imagine our ponytail ends dragging on the ground as we do our fabulous handstands, or as we lie on the soft dirt ground, counting the clouds in the sky.

Serious playtime•••

And what kid can resist crawling under the bed — no need for dusting, kids' hair will do the job. Tackle football in the mud, oh yeah! Oh, and did I mention how we kids like to play in each other's hair with our dirty little hands. (We're still learning to wash our hands so we don't spread germs.) These are just a few things that we do in a day of play that can dirty and mess up our hair.

Our own style•••

We don't work in professional places. We go to school, so we have our own hairdos to express ourselves.

Tangled Hair

There's nothing worse than getting tangled hair. We believe in prevention, so here's what to do to keep from tangling our hair and what to do when it's too late.

- Rubbing and scrubbing our hair in circular motions during a shampoo will cause our hair to tangle.

- Rushing and combing big sections of thick hair at the root area first can cause hair tangles.

- Not combing our hair thoroughly, *before* shampooing, can cause tangles.

- Gels and the pink stuff can build up on our hair, causing tangles.

- Not combing the hair underneath. (Grown-ups, it might be faster to top comb, but when you comb the hair underneath, it will tangle and hurt.)

Removing tangles from kids' hair:

1. Work with small sections of hair, gently separating the hair with your fingers.

2. Comb in a plucking manner to loosen the intermingled hairs. (Don't pull on the tangles because they will tighten.)
 After removing braids, if the hair is dry and tangled, spray a mist of water on each small section to soften the hair and make it comb out easily.

Time to Trim Split Hair Ends

By age four it's time to trim our hair ends. This helps make our hair easy to comb and keeps it from tangling.

- Ages 4 -10 trim once a year,
- Ages 11 -16 trim twice a year (if needed).

The texture and condition of our hair will tell you if the ends need trimming. For example, it's time to trim the ends if our hair tangles while combing, forms hair balls or looks uneven, dull and ashy. Permed or relaxed hair will need to be trimmed more often, because the chemical dries out the ends.

You can have a hair stylist trim the ends or do it yourself, if you think you can do it without messing it up. **Just trim 1/4 to 1/2 inch off the ends.** (Caution — If you cut off too much, the hair ends will be too even to braid or twist.)

How to trim 1/4 - 1/2 inch from the hair ends:

1. Shampoo, condition, comb-out and blow dry the hair smooth.

2. Part from front to back and ear to ear, to make four sections.

3. Make 1-inch horizontal partings within each section, comb the hair downward and trim 1/4 -1/2 inch off the ends.

A kids' shampoo is easy if you have the right stuff. Combs, towels, shampoo, conditioner and a blow-dryer with comb nozzle.

Keeping Kids' Hair Clean and Soft

Shampooing and conditioning keeps our hair soft and clean. It's
good to shampoo our hair at least every two weeks,
to keep it conditioned and easy to comb.

First, gather two thick towels, a large tooth comb, *Cornrows & Co.
shampoo and conditioner, and a blow dryer with a comb nozzle.

Second, choose a comfortable place to do the shampoo. Small kids can
lay on their backs on the kitchen counter, with the head tilted in the sink.
Be sure to cushion the neck with thick towels. Older kids can stand and
hold the head downward into the sink or bathtub.

Now, you're ready to do a 6-Step kids' shampoo:

1. Comb the hair out thoroughly, then rinse the hair with warm
water for a few minutes.
2. Apply *shampoo to the scalp and ends of the hair. Massage the
scalp with in and out motions, pulling the lather out to the ends.
3. Rinse thoroughly for a long time.
4. Apply *conditioner to the hair, section and comb it through to
the hair ends. (This is important to make the hair soft.)
5. Rinse (or leave on conditioner), then comb out and twist the hair
into 6 to 15 sections depending on how thick and long the hair is.
6. Wait 30 minutes, then blow-dry smooth and comb the hair into
your favorite style. (Blow dry is recommended for thick hair.)

After the shampoo comb out, always blow-dry hair with a comb nozzle attachment. Do not let thick hair air dry, then attempt to style or braid it. The hair will be difficult to comb and it will hurt. OUCH!

To Section and Blow-Dry Thick Natural Hair

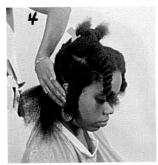

1. Part the hair into small, easy-to-comb sections. Use your fingers to separate the hair.

2. Hold the section close to the scalp. Start combing the ends first then comb down to the scalp hair.

3. Divide the combed-out section in two and twist the two pieces together to keep the hair separated & organized.

4. Using a comb nozzle, blow-dry each section. Dry the ends first, then dry the hair down to the scalp.

For extra care, do a quick *Cornrows & Co. Hot-Oil or Deep Conditioner every other month. This will keep kids' hair in good condition and prevent product build-up on the hair.

Conditioner is lotion for the hair. It keeps hair soft, gives it sheen and makes it easy to comb after a shampoo. Always apply a condition rinse after a shampoo. Comb the *conditioner or natural hair oil through the hair to coat every strand.

- If the hair feels brittle and crunchy, condition with hot oil.

- If the hair and scalp look dry and ashy, deep condition for moisture.

Cornrows & Co. Quick Hot-Oil Conditioner
If the hair is very soiled, shampoo once.
1. Apply about 1/2 oz. of Cornrows & Co. Natural Hair Oil to the hair.
2. Wrap a moist warm towel around the hair for 15 minutes.
3. Comb the warmed oil through the hair and massage into the scalp.
4. Shampoo the hair thoroughly to remove all of the oil.
5. Apply Cornrows & Co. Sweet Orange Conditioner, rinse, comb out, blow dry (optional) and style.

Cornrows & Co. Deep Conditioner
1. Shampoo twice with Cornrows & Co. shampoo.
2. Part the hair into eight sections (more if the hair is very thick or long).
3. Apply conditioner and comb it through each section of the hair.
4. Wrap a moist warm towel around the hair for 15 minutes.
5. Rinse thoroughly, comb out, blow-dry and style.

We don't cry when you comb our hair.

10 Reasons Kids Let Someone Else Do Their Hair And Why They Don't Cry

Grown-ups, don't take it too personally when we smile, sit still and don't cry a tear when a sister, cousin, baby-sitter or someone else does our hair. Just think of it as a helping hand from the village, because it takes a village to care for our hair. Here are some reasons why we might act different when someone else does our hair:

1. It doesn't hurt when they do it.
2. They put the fear of God in us.
3. We like them and enjoy spending that special time with them.
4. They are never in a hurry, so the hairstyle looks nice when it's finished.
5. They let us choose our styles.
6. We just prefer to have our hair combed any other time than a school-day morning or late at night.
7. When they volunteer to do it, it really needs to be done.
8. After they finish our hair, they let us do the "mirror dance."
9. Their breath doesn't stink when they are doing a close-up bang.
10. They don't use their spit to smooth our hairline.

It's fun making the hair into a pretty Bun.

Easy Styles that Grown-Ups Can Do

All of the styles in this section of the book are easy styles. They are very simple to do and eventually when kids become older, they will be able to do their own hair. Teens can do Teen-A-Rama styles because they have manual dexterity. WOW — that's a big word. Manual dexterity means strong hands that can comb, swirl, twist and twirl the hair.

I can curl and twirl my own hair.

Girlie Curls

Now this twist style is ready for playtime or anytime.

1. Shampoo, condition, and blow-dry (optional) the hair.
2. Divide small pieces of the hair in two and twist the two pieces together.
3. Roll the twist on soft sponge rollers or paper towel rollers.

Paper Towel Rollers: Roll a sheet of paper towel into a tube shape. Roll the hair onto the paper towel, the same as a roller, then tie the ends together to hold the roller onto the hair.

"My hair is soft like cotton, puffs like popcorn and stands high like a princess crown.

Xenia Afro Puff

Soft and cottony, like cotton candy.

1. Shampoo, condition and softly blow-dry the hair with a nozzle comb.

2. Use a circular comb barrette to make the Afro puff.

3. To keep the Afro puff soft and easy to comb, at bedtime comb the hair into two cornrows then cover with a scarf. In the morning, take out the cornrows and style the hair into Xenia Afro Puffs.

"Smart Girl Upcurls"

Twist Wet Set

1. To make twist wet set curls, individually twist the hair.
2. Roll three twists on small rollers until the hair dries.
3. Remove the rollers and place the twist curls in your favorite style.

The curls will last until you shampoo the hair again.

Grown-Ups Do Some Strange Things

Kids are always watching grown-ups to see what they do next, because they know better. But sometimes grown-ups confuse us because they say one thing and they do the opposite. They mean what they say, but they don't know what they do.
Sound confusing? It is to a kid.

Grown-ups sometimes can send mixed-up messages.
- They straighten their curly hair, but tell us not to straighten our curly hair.
- They accuse kids of being tender-headed, but they comb our hair like a tug of war.
- They teach us to be proud of ourselves, but they say not so proud things about our hair.

Do as I say. Do as I do. Look at me look at you!

Individual Twists

1. Shampoo, condition and blow dry (optional) the hair.

2. Divide small sections of the hair in two, then rope twist the two pieces together.

3. Wet the ends of the twist to form coily curls.

4. This style can be shampooed with the twists in.

Do not keep the same twists in more than three weeks or the hair will tangle.

What's a kid to do?

Sometimes It Hurts

Sometimes it hurts... when we have our hair combed. It may hurt because the grown-up combing or braiding our hair is learning how to do it better. So, we must help them by teaching them the do's and don'ts of combing our hair.

Sometimes it hurts... because we don't sit perfectly still. If we don't move our heads, it's a lot easier for grown-ups to comb our hair and not hurt us.

Sometimes it hurts... because grown-ups are in a hurry. When they are rushing they pull, yank and hold our hair too tight. Grown-ups, slow down and plan a good time to do our hair.

Sometimes it hurts... because we think it will hurt. But it won't hurt if we know it's just a thought that it will hurt. And maybe one time it did hurt, but that doesn't mean it's gonna hurt now. I think if grown-ups read this book, they'll learn how not to hurt, and then we won't think it will hurt and, by gosh, it won't hurt!

Twist Pogtails

Easy as 1 - 2 - 3

1. Part the hair into three sections. Secure with band holders.

2. Make three twist pogtails with each section.

3. Put my favorite barrettes on the ends.

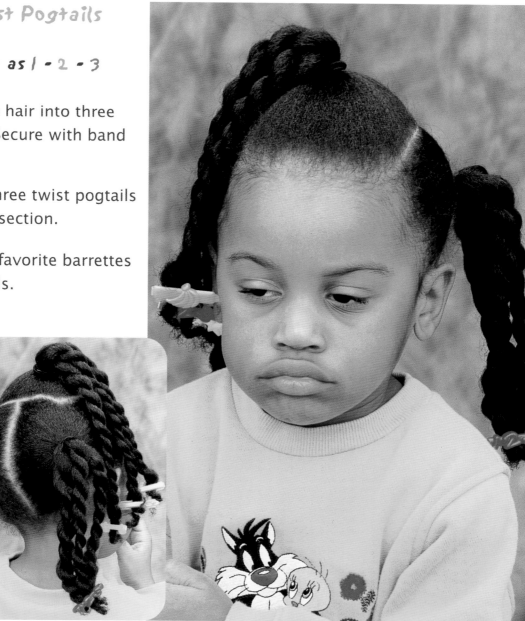

I'm wearing Afro Buns. Did you know, they are soft, spongy and can stand up on their own?

I wanna dance under the sun when my hair is in a Honey-Bun.
Oh... when I get the great hairstyle I like,
I am so happy it makes me feel alright.

Like a road map to heaven, follow the criss-cross
braids to the top of my head.

Criss-Cross Braids

Looks hard to do, but its only eight cornrows. Make two cornrows cross each other.

1. Part the hair into four equal pie sections.

2. Part each pie section into four parts; top to bottom, side to side.

Point is the top of head. ➤

3. **Start** cornrow at section 4 and cross over into section 1. Then cornrow section 3 across into section 2.

4. Do this for all four pie sections, then gather together on top of my head.

Simple Cornrows

Five inside cornrows to the top of my head.

Five outside cornrows to the top of my head.

School Daze Cornrows

This style is for grown-ups who know how to braid, but need style ideas.

. Cornrow the back section downward.
. Make an angled side part from the front to the opposite back ear.
3. Cornrow away from the face on an angle, and make a beaded cornrow bang.

I was supposed to have cornrows but I wanted freedom hair!

Making cornrows is as easy as one - two - three.
Try it and you will see.

Making Cornrows is easy as 1 - 2 - 3

1. Divide a section of hair into three pieces,
   outer left - middle - outer right

2. To braid, put the outer right piece over the middle,
   then the middle piece becomes the outer right.

3. Put the outer left piece over the middle and
   the middle piece becomes the outer left.

Keep doing these 1 - 2 - 3 steps and you are braiding.
Don't think about it too hard, just let your fingers feel the rhythm.
To make a cornrow, add the hair of the long section into the
outer pieces as you are braiding.

Over the middle for a overhand cornrow like I am wearing.
Under the middle for a flat inverted cornrow.

Make small partings and plait the hair to the ends.

Simple plaits, simply marvelous.

Sisters love each other forever.

Do Kids Need Hair Extensions ?

There are three reasons grown-ups put hair extensions in kids' hair.

1. To make a kid's style last a long time.
2. To cover or hold a style for hair that has been damaged.
3. To add hair length.

Kids do not need hair extensions, especially if you take care of our natural hair. It's okay as a style change, but it's not good for young kids. Hair extensions can take a long time to put in and a long time to take out.

If you are adding extensions to make our hairstyle last longer, sorry. Extension styles do not last much longer on small kids because our soft hair will frizz out of the extension. Wait until we are about seven years old. And if we wear extension styles too much, our scalps will feel tender-headed when you comb our hair.

Since long hair extensions are so noticeable, keep the length no more than two inches past our natural hair. Don't make us feel insecure about our natural hair length. Hair does not have to be long to be pretty.   Also, be sure to have it done by an experienced, professional hair braider. Please don't try to do it yourself or have the girl next door's cousin experiment on our hair. Too tight braids and heavy extensions are a common problem with inexperienced hair braiders. It could be a painful, unforgettable experience that could lead to hair damage and embarrassment, as with Shuletta.

One day Shuletta's mom put a kiddie perm in her hair and the perm burned out a big spot of hair. Her mom, who had long braids, cut off one of her own braids and sewed it to the missing spot on Shuletta's head. All Shuletta remembers is that she was terrified of that sewn-on braid. She was afraid to move her head because the braid could fall off. Imagine being afraid to move your head!

Another time Shuletta's mom permed her hair, then combed it all to the top and pinned on a big bush ball. Shuletta remembers a boy classmate who liked her and chased her home from school. She said she ran sooo fast because her bush ball extension was falling off, and she didn't want him to catch her and see her bush ball fall off her head.

Shuletta remembers hair extensions that made her ashamed and afraid to move her head.

All of the kids in the book have natural styles with no extensions. We don't need extensions to make our hair pretty. Love our natural hair and teach us to love and appreciate it, too.

(Note to grown-ups——if extension braids are too tight and painful, remove them immediately.)

Getting older is fun and our hair styles should show it. Don't ya know it.

Teen - A- Rama Styles

Becoming a teen-ager is exciting because we make a rite of passage from kid to big kid. When we get a little older, we want a hairstyle that expresses our new teenhood. No more baby-looking hair styles and we definitely don't want to look like a grown-up. But we must learn to take care of our hair without perms and relaxers so that we can keep our beautiful teen hair. Most teenagers ruin their natural hair by age sixteen, because they straighten it. We don't need perms or chemical straighteners to look good. In the teen-a-rama section, you'll see some cool, fly hairdos. Just pay attention . . .

First, learn how to keep your hair clean and conditioned.

Second, practice three natural hair styles you can do yourself.

Third, don't use chemicals to straighten your hair, unless you want broken-off hair and short edges. That's definitely not cute!

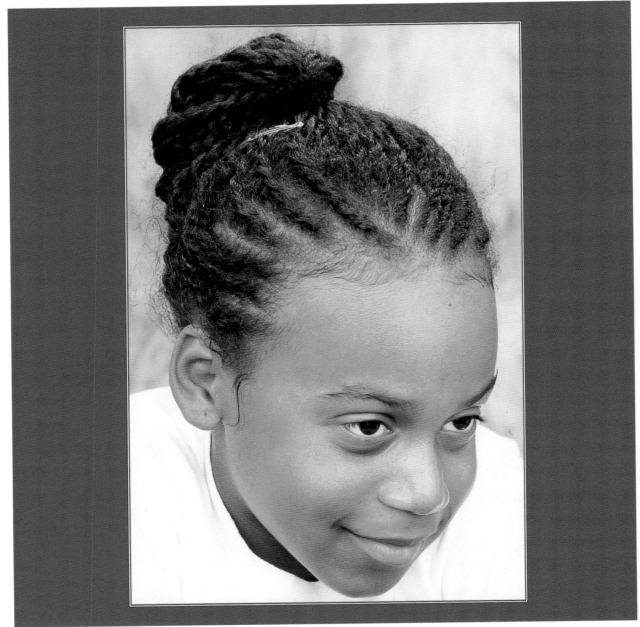

Twist-out in the back and cornrows in the front.
Pull up to make a neat bun on top.

Wear your own style, be your own person.

Fly Girl — Young Look

• Choose a hairstyle that's good for your face shape and doesn't make you look grown-up and old.

• Don't try to make your hair into something it's not, or you'll only end up ruining it. If it's naturally curly don't try to make it straight, and if its naturally straight, don't force it to be curly.

• If all your friends have permed hair and you feel peer pressure to straighten yours, choose a safe way to do it:
        To straighten naturally curly hair, try a press and curl or get thin braids or micro twists for a sleek, smooth look.
        To curl or wave naturally straight hair, make large tight stitch braids or twists while the hair is wet. After the hair completely dries, unbraid it and you will have wavy curly hair. These styles will last until you shampoo the hair again.

• Be your own person. Don't choose hair styles just because your friends are wearing them. Create your own natural style.

• Your hair says who you are and who you wanna be. What does your hair say about you?

Love yourself, love your hair, love life.

Make tiny, individual twists and roll the ends loosely.

Eat fruits and vegetables for healthy hair.

Naturally curly hair you can wash and wear.

Handrolls, waves and twists. Take your pick of boy styles.

Boys, Boys, Boys

Seems like the girls got most of the pages. We know ladies come first, but we need hair care, too! Our hair care is not very different except for haircuts and boy styles. We shampoo the same, condition the same and, of course, brush and oil our scalps the same as everyone else. The sections in this book that explain how to condition, shampoo and other stuff is for our hair, too. Boys wear locks, twists, handrolls, braids, cornrows and Afros. So you see, we have something to say here.

Barber Shop Time •••

Our first haircut is real important. Wait until we are about one or two years old. Never cut our hair too close or too soon because it can damage the hair roots. The first haircut should be done with scissors, because they are quieter and our scalps cannot be damaged by cutting our hair too low. Also, we need to feel comfortable. Choose a friendly barber who likes kids, will give us a first-time tour of the barber shop, and will let us hold the clippers and combs. The barber should have experience with kids because we move our heads a lot and may cry a little.

My hair protects my head and keeps it warm. So don't cut it all at once. Leave at least one inch of hair on my first haircut. Oh, it may be a good idea to show me a picture of a boy with a haircut, so I'll know what's happening and can give my opinion about whether I'm ready for my first haircut. If my hair is very soft and has big curls, it's best to always use scissors to cut my hair. Clippers can make me look like a scared chicken.

If you decide to do the haircut, be sure not to cut too close and keep the clipper blade set at the factory setting. It's important that at home, parents practice good sanitation. Buy spray disinfectant or 91% proof alcohol to clean the clippers.

Choose a barber who sterilizes his tools and combs after each haircut. Watch the person getting a haircut before you, to see if the barber washes his hands and cleans his tools. Germs and scalp diseases like ringworm can be spread by not cleaning combs and barber tools.

As we get older (six years), we can try close cuts, fades, lines and "cool boy" haircuts. It's important that the barber not trim back into the front hairline because our hair looks raggedy as it grows out. To avoid hair bumps, never cut our hair too close with an over-lapping blade. If the blade is not properly set, it will cut into our skin, causing irritation and bumps. Never cut our hair with a face razor.

A good hair cut will last about three weeks and won't cause bumps or scalp problems. Boys with haircuts can shampoo their hair every three days.

Growing My "Bush" •••

Grown-ups get worried when they see boys growing an Afro bush. It's cool — it won't hurt you. We like to grow hair, too. The important thing is that we keep it combed daily, and if we get the neckline shaped up, it will look neat while its growing high. When it gets long, we'll pick it out with an Afro pick then pat it in shape with our hands. When it grows really long, it's a good idea to braid it at night to keep it soft and easy to comb. When it's combed perfect, it looks like an art sculpture. Grown-ups, be open-minded and let us boys wear "freedom hair."

Three Things to Do for a Neat Afro Bush

1. Keep it combed every day.
2. Mist it with water, and rub some oil on it to comb it easily.
3. Shampoo it once a week.

Boys' Twists & Locks •••

Once I grow an Afro bush, I will have enough hair for twists. My hair must be three inches long and not trimmed evenly. Twists are great because they look like locks, but they are not permanent. You can take out twists and put them back in.

To lock the hair, leave the hair twisted and never comb it out. Shampoo every week, separate the new hair growth, then handroll the locks

It's not what's on my head. It's what's in it.
Being smart starts with being proud.

to keep them smooth and neat at the scalp. It takes months for the hair to start locking but once it locks, it will lock neat and strong.

Keeping It Real •••

A good haircut makes all the difference. A good haircut combs in place and always looks neat even after a serious game of basketball.
What can I say...but get a good haircut.

Making Waves •••

Kinky, curly, nappy hair can make strong waves. Use a medium bristle brush and a natural pomade oil. The size of the curl or kink in our natural hair will make little or big waves.

Shampoo or wet the hair, rub on a natural pomade oil, then brush and brush and brush, at least 25 times every day. Do this each morning to keep the waves neat and fresh looking. Be sure to shampoo and condition the hair every week.

Now you see we care about our hair, too. We just need to know what to do. We can wear our hair long, twisted, locked, faded, braided and shaved bald. The most important thing is that we take good care of it and keep it neat and well-groomed. After all, every girl likes a well-groomed boy.

Style on opposite page: Handrolls

Honor Your Ancestors. Respect yourself.

Think Power! Think Positive!

Hair Locks

Hair Locks are "culturally cool." They are formed by twisting two pieces of the natural hair together. Once the hair is twisted, it's left to grow and intertwine into permanent hair locks. When you lock your hair, it will grow very long over the years. You can shampoo your hair as usual and not have to spend a lot of time doing your hair. Locks can be curled, waved and worn in so many fly styles. This is a hair choice for the brave, confident and culturally collected teen-a-rama kid. And we don't worry what people have to say about our terrific locks, because some folks understand and others just don't get it.

We wear them with pride!

Hair locks this length take up to four years to grow.

Locks can be shampooed and styled in many looks, but they cannot be combed out. So be real. Be sure.

Nu-locks are locks less than six months old.

Short & Sassy Nu-Locks

Starting Locks

1. Individually twist the natural hair.

2. Do not use gels or beeswax. The hair's natural kink will hold the twist together.

3. Shampoo every week with Cornrows & Co. Lock Shampoo.

4. For maintenance, separate and hand-roll the new hair growth every four to six weeks.

5. Once the hair locks, condition it after every shampoo.

It can take up to six months for the hair to begin locking. Be patient!

You make your own happiness every day.

Phat Plaits

1. Shampoo, condition and blow dry (optional) the hair.

2. Make diamond shaped parts, then braid overhand so that the base is flat.

3. Tightly roll ends on sponge rollers.

Close your eyes, hold your nose and jump in!

Swimmers' Hair Care

Kids look forward to wet and wild water fun. Wave chasing at the beach, dancing in the fire hydrant, lawn sprinkler tag games, and good old-fashioned swimming like a fish. Can't imagine doing water fun and can't get your hair wet? Grown-ups may know how to swim without getting their hair wet (dog paddle or toe testing), but kids must get wet from head to toe. We know just what to do to keep our hair in good shape — during the water fun and once it's over.

- Wear a swim cap when swimming in chlorinated water.

- Select the right products to keep your hair moist and conditioned.

- Rinse your hair thoroughly after swimming in chlorinated pools and sandy salt-water beaches.

- Choose water friendly hair styles like twists, cornrows, and individual braids. Water friendly hair styles can be rinsed every time without combing.

- Extension styles become heavy when wet and take longer to dry, so use very little extension (1/2 pack) and do simple styles.

My hair loves water. It curls, coils and stays in style.

■ To remove beach sand from your hair, use a blow dryer on cool temperature and blow the sand out of the hair. Be sure to blow the sand away from the eyes.

■ Chlorine can be very drying to the hair and cause the hair color to fade and appear ashy and dull. To prevent overexposure to chlorine water, saturate the hair with *conditioner, then cover it with a swim cap and rinse after swimming. (If the hairline is the only area that gets wet, then put the *conditioner only on the hairline area.)

■ Re-do swimmers' hair styles at least every two weeks. If you leave the hair twisted or braided for months, the frequent wetting may cause it to tangle and lock at the root. This can damage the hair and will hurt when you comb it out.

■ Do a Cornrows & Co. Hot Oil Conditioner once a month (see page 21). And after each swim, apply Cornrows & Co. Sweet Orange Conditioner, then rinse thoroughly to keep your hairstyle soft and fresh looking.

■ Become an Olympic swimmer — you can do it!

BEADS, BOWS, BARRETTES & BANGS

Our Ancestors loved colorful clothes, beads, body adornment and hair stuff. We feel their vibrations and their sense of style.

Beads, barrettes, bands, bangs and hair stuff are too cool to talk about. You just have to do it. There are no rules — just do what makes you feel good. Use them to add color, pizazz and spice to a plain hairdo.

Grown-ups, please let us choose the bows, barrettes and beads we'd like to wear. We really know what we like and what makes us feel wonderful. Also, it's not absolutely important that our hair stuff match our clothes because we have our own cultural style. It's called color-style. The more colors we wear, the more power we gain — GERONIMO !

Beads make music in my ears. They tinkle, clinkle and clickety clack.

Make it fun and funky with hair barrettes.

Bangs and
Beads

Beads and
Bangs

An African Queen BANG

The hair rite of passage for girls is wearing bangs. All girls want bangs! But we have to wait until grown-ups say it's okay to have hair flopping in our faces.

But once they say its okay — bangs are it. They are fun, mysterious hide-behinds that make us feel like the African queen, Cleopatra. There are so many ways to wear them — front bangs, side bangs, beaded, straight, curly and Afro bush bangs. Guess what, if grown-ups don't want you to cut your hair into bangs, you can wear a Cornrows & Co. Faux Bang, just like me. (Faux means fake.)

Ponytails, etc.

One of the easiest hairstyles kids can do is a ponytail. You can make one, two, three or as many as you can get on your head.

Make them low, high, on the side, in the middle or all over. A ponytail is long, an Afro puff is fluffy, a bunnytail is round and a pigtail is small. Which one can you make?

Ouch...don't pull too tight, it will make your head ache and your eyes stretch.

Side Show

Not too tight!

Low Rider

Middle Road

This style has individual twists in the back and flat twists in the front.

1. Pull the hair together into a ponytail.

2. Make two braids and pin in place.

I feel pretty today. Do you?

Natural hair is everywhere; take a look around.

Two-braid ponytails.

It's not pigtails.
It's not ponytails.
It's not pogtails.
It's Afro puffs.

Easy as 1-2-3

1. Part the hair into three sections.

2. Secure each section with a ponytail holder.

3. Fluff each puff with your fingers.

For smooth, shiny curls, do a twist wet set.
See page 29 for how-to.

Africa is in my hair. It's in my soul and my whole body.

My natural hair was blow dried with a comb nozzle. It's healthy, natural, smooth and easy to comb. When I wet it, it will spring back to its beautiful, "nap-tural" curl. So you see, no kiddie perm for me!

No Chemicals In Kids' Hair!

There are two reasons grown-ups relax or perm kids' hair.

1. They don't like our curly nap-tural hair.
2. They think a chemical straightener will make it easy to comb.

There are two reasons kids want a relaxer perm.

1. All of our friends have one.
2. Other kids make fun of our beautiful, curly nap-tural hair.

There are two reasons kids do not need relaxer perms.

1. *They're poison.* Relaxers, kiddie perms, no lye perms, etc., are caustic, toxic chemicals that are absorbed into our skin. It's like slowly poisoning us. Relaxer perms have sodium hydroxide lye, the same chemical used to unclog sink drains. Did you know that African- American kids are the only children that toxic hair chemicals are made for? Why are grown-ups so eager to buy them? Perhaps they don't know the danger and harm it will cause to our health.

2. *It breaks the hair off short.* The relaxer perm is a dissolver and with constant use it slowly dissolves and melts the hair. The hair eventually becomes weak and thin. Even though the straightened hair is easy to comb, it breaks off when the curly new hair grows back. Once you put chemicals on kids' hair, it takes more than a year to grow back a full head of healthy natural hair.

Kids are born with beautiful hair, but grown-ups ruin it for life when they get us hooked on straightened hair. You can blow-dry our hair smooth, so please, NO KIDDIE PERMS.

Healthy hair starts with a healthy diet, cleanliness
and natural products. If we learn to take care of
our hair and our health,
we will grow up with good hair.

Good Hair

Good Hair

Is Healthy Hair,

Clean Hair,

Beautiful Hair,

For Life.

Kids' Hair & Scalp Problems

Several things can cause hair breakage, rashes, dandruff and other kids' hair problems. Some of these problems are caused by mistakes, bad hair care, sickness, and contagion. The good news is that all of our hair and scalp problems can be taken care of, if grown-ups know what to do.

Caused by Mistakes

Bubble Gum in Hair...

This hair problem is troublesome when it happens, but it can be easily taken care of. The best way to prevent it is not to chew gum. If kids do chew gum, we should keep it inside our mouths. We shouldn't stretch it with our fingers. And we definitely shouldn't go to sleep with it! However, if we do get gum in our hair, here's what to do:

First, put ice cubes in a plastic bag. Hold it on our gummy hair until the gum freezes and hardens.

Second, once the gum is hardened, carefully break and peel it away from our hair. Voila! Gumless hair.

No matter how frustrated you get, do not put my head in the freezer.

Surprise Hair Cut •••

Kids are curious and sometimes we do not know the consequences of the things we do. Usually, when we are under the age of six, we don't understand that if we cut off a braid or a plug of hair, it can't be put back on.

Cutting off just one ponytail or braid does not leave grown-ups with a lot of styling options. Usually the area is too large to cover. Or it's in a bizarre spot, and we can't comb the long hair over it.

So here's what to do:

One, cut all the hair down to the shortest length and style in a pretty Afro with barrettes or handrolls (see below).

Two, if the cut-off section of hair is at least three inches, you can have a professional braider add an extension to the short area to make it blend with the other hair.

Tiara's dad is a barber. She cut off her braid just like Daddy cuts hair. Now she has a new hair style. The good news is — the hair will grow back.

Caused by Bad Hair Care

Lint in Hair •••

I remember this little girl who had lint balls in her hair. When she washed her hair, and even when she combed it, the lint balls would not comb out. Well, guess what? The lint was sticking to her hair because her mom was using the wrong kind of hair oil. Her mom was using petroleum grease. This is made from the same kind of oil that is used in your car! Petroleum grease is heavy and does not easily wash away. So if you don't want lint balls in our hair, don't use hair grease made with petroleum or mineral oil. The best hair oils are natural oils like shea butter, jojoba oil, coconut oil and royal jelly. Natural oils will keep our hair soft, shiny and lint free.

Knotted Hair Ends •••

When this happens it means our hair ends need to be trimmed. A trim does not hurt our hair. It just snips away the worn-out ends. And you'll see that once you clip the ends, the hair will be easier to comb.

Dry Scalp & Dandruff •••

Kids typically should not have dandruff or dry scalp. If you notice dandruff or a flaky scalp, try the following:
- Shampoo the hair more often (every five days) and thoroughly.
- Change to natural hair care products made for your kid's hair type.
- Rinse the hair with a warm organic apple cider vinegar rinse.
- Put castor oil on the dry areas before shampooing.
- Do not use petroleum or mineral oil on the scalp.
- If the scalp has scabs of patchy dandruff, apply the Pamferrell Scaly Scalp Tonic and shampoo every four days. (For very thick hair, do individual twists and shampoo the hair with the twists in.)

Dry Hair & Shedding ●●●

 If you notice our hair is dry, dull looking and sheds a lot, these may be the possible causes:

- Poor hygiene, infrequent shampooing and conditioning, wrong products.
- Malnutrition (poor diet), fast food, crash diets.
- Anemia (iron deficiency)
- No fresh fruits or vegetables each day, and too little protein.
- Too many carbohydrates (sweets, breads, pizza, pasta, sugar)
- Anorexia nervosa (eating disorder)

Traction Alopecia ●●●

This type of hair loss usually shows up along the hairline and looks like a smooth bald area. It's often caused by too much pulling and hairstyles that are too tight. For example, elastic bands, tight braids, kiddie perms, tight barrettes, hot combing, tight rollers and hard gel cause thin hairlines. Trying to make our hair look smooth and straight by pulling it too tight can scar the hair follicle and cause our hair to stop growing.

Oh My! Broken Hair Edges ●●●

Hair edges are where the face stops and the hair begins. This is where short hair blends into long hair. Sometimes the hair edges can break off, and the short hairs don't blend into the long hairs because some hair is missing. Here are three things that cause broken hair edges:

One, kiddie perm hair straightener. It burns and melts our hair away until eventually our edges bald. We'd rather have naturally curly, nappy hair edges than no edges at all.

Two, pulling or braiding the hair too tight. You can tell our hair is pulled too tight if pimples appear along the part or hair edge, or we make kooky faces.

Three, pressing our hair with a hot comb. Heat stretches the hair out of shape, making it weak and causing it to break easily. Just blow it dry with a comb nozzle and that will make it easy to comb and style. Press our clothes, not our hair!

Chemical Hair Breakage •••

Breakage from a perm relaxer starts where the curly new hair growth meets the chemically straightened hair. The best way to grow our natural hair back is to have it professionally braided until the permed hair can be cut off. Shampoo and condition the braids regularly to keep the hair soft. Do not give a chemical touch-up to stop breakage. This caused the breakage, so it will *not* stop it. If anyone suggests a chemical touch-up, they are wrong!

Caused by Sickness

Alopecia Areata •••

If a kid gets alopecia, smooth circular bald spots will suddenly appear throughout the scalp. Alopecia can be caused by an autoimmune problem. Autoimmune means that our antibodies and defense mechanisms get confused and start to attack the good cells and tissues in our bodies. This causes destruction and inflammation to hair tissues. Depending on a kid's overall health, alopecia areata spots may grow back in 3 -12 months. Alopecia is also linked to a biotin deficiency. Here are some things that may help:

- Biocytin (can be purchased at the health food store).
- Brewer's yeast, cauliflower, rice bran, oatmeal bran.
- Vegetarian diet (plenty of raw green vegetables) or one with fish too.
- Vitamin B complex and co-enzyme Q10 (antioxidant).
- Flaxseed oil (fatty essential acid), taken daily.
- Proper food combinations to help food digestion, since biotin is destroyed by gut bacteria.

- Antibiotics may lower biotin levels because they also destroy gut bacteria.
- Some dermatologists may suggest steriod shots to the bald spots. This may make some hair grow, but steroids are toxic and they don't deal with the cause of the problem, so the condition will reappear.

A healthy diet, wholistic therapy and good hair care will help to improve alopecia areata. Shampoo and condition our hair at least every five days. Massage the Pamferrell Follicle Fortifier on the affected areas.

Scalp treatments are also recommended. If there are more than two bald patches and they do not grow in after six months, seek the help of a nutritionist or naturopath doctor.

Trichotillomania or Hair Pulling •••

This is a psychological disorder usually seen in kids. It's a form of traction alopecia caused by an unconscious habit of rubbing or pulling the hair. The constant rubbing, plucking or pulling causes the hair to break down to a stubble. Pulling on the hair long-term can scar the hair follicle, which can lead to baldness. Here are some suggested treatments:

- Psychotherapy.
- Nutritional program to bring balance to your kid's overall health.
- Hairstyle that contains the hair, to prevent your child from pulling it.
- Helping your kid become conscious of his or her behavior and replacing that behavior with other activities.

Caused by Touching an Infected Thing or Person
(Caution — these problems are contagious. Use gloves.)

Head Lice •••

This is a highly contagious animal parasite that infests the hair and scalp. It can be passed on by standing close to someone who is infested, and by using the same combs, brushes, pillows, hats, public seats and anything that makes contact with the eggs (nits) or the louse (bug).

Kids are more likely to get this hair bug by accidental contact with other kids who have it. It's a good habit to check your kid's hair daily to make sure there are no signs of head lice. If left undisturbed the lice will multiply rapidly. Once the head lice get in the hair, they lay eggs that hatch within two to three days.

What do they look like? The eggs (nits) look like dandruff but they don't brush off the hair because the lice spread a gluey substance that sticks the nits to the hair.

Rub your gloved fingers over the white flakes and if the flakes don't move, they're nits. The head lice are grayish-colored, very tiny bugs with six legs. If you open the hair and look closely, you'll see the bugs move quickly to hide within the hair close to the scalp.

One way to tell if kids have head lice is by our constant scratching. The lice feed on the scalp blood, causing intense itching. Scratching can cause sores or irritation. So make sure we don't scratch too much.

Hair salons cannot treat head lice infestation, so it's important that you understand how to kill head lice and destroy nits.

Preparation. Wear gloves, cover your hair with a plastic cap and wear a long-sleeved shirt.

To kill the head lice (suffocate them):
1. Shampoo with *Cornrows & Co. Natural Head Lice Shampoo. (Head lice have become resistant to the chemical head lice shampoos.)
2. Pour vinegar through the hair. Saturate every strand with this rinse.
3. Part the hair in small sections. Saturate with Cornrows & Co. Head Lice Oil.
4. Cover the head with a plastic cap for an hour.
5. Wipe the oil from the hair with paper towels (discard).
6. Rinse with hot water, then shampoo twice with the *Head Lice Shampoo.
7. Section, comb out and blow dry the hair smooth.

To destroy the nits (apply heat to the hair):
1. Spread a white sheet on the floor under the child.
2. Give a hot-comb hard press to make the hair very straight.
3. Make very thin, small sections and comb through each strand of hair with a fine-tooth head lice comb. The remaining head lice will comb out on the white sheet. (Wash sheet with hot water and bleach.)

▪ Repeat this entire process two more times in three-day intervals, to be sure the head lice and nits are destroyed. Be sure to wash all pillow cases, hats, and anything that's had contact with the hair. Check other family members to be sure no one else in your household has head lice.

▪ Cut the hair off of boys and all kids with locks! It's impossible to destroy lice in locked or braided hair because you must be able to comb the hair strands.

- After a head lice treatment, put a few drops of lavender essential oil on your brush and combs.

- Notify your kid's school or other places where he or she made contact with kids.

Ringworm [Tinea] •••

Note: See a pediatrician or dermatologist for rash, pimples or open sores.

This is a fungoid parasite infection that a kid can get in showers, baths, swimming pools or by touching an infected person. It's round and about the size of a nickel or larger. And it has slightly raised red pimples or blisters on the outer edge. The way you can tell a ringworm from a rash is that the center heals as the ringworm spreads outward. Like head lice, a case of ringworm causes intense itching.

Ringworm home remedies suggested by elder grown-ups:
- Put crushed raw garlic on the affected area, then cover with a gauze bandage that allows air to penetrate. Don't use plastic or an air-tight bandage that seals in dampness. If the ringworm is damp, it won't heal.

- Mix 1 tablespoon bleach with 3 tablespoons water. Apply with a cotton ball to the affected area. Leave on for 30 minutes then rinse with cool water. *(Use rubber gloves, discard after use and disinfect any combs or materials you come in contact with.)*

Beauty

Beauty is only skin deep,
at least that's what people say,
but things are sort of different,
in this society today.
People look at beauty as a reflection of
what they see,
but if that is all they are looking at,
they really don't see me.
Dig a little deeper to know a person well,
and if you're digging deep enough,
you just might find yourself!

Jeannine Ferrell, age 14

The End

Kids Talk Hair..........

Afia Hemphill
Afra Abdullah
Alexa Haile (cover)
Alexander Ojo
Amber Ferrell
Annie Baines
Audrey Haile (cover)
Dante Ferrell Maynard
Gloria Ojo
Isaac M. Purcelle (infant)
Jordanna Bradley
Kamila Mack
Khadijah El (infant)
Kierra Hargett
Madaya Duggins
Mark Robert Johnson
Micheal Jerome Lester
Marc Jeffers
Mariama Roe-Wills
Mazare Braswell
Nia Pride
Patrice Rodgers
Raven Jeffers
Raven Trimble
Sharay Vaughn
Simone S. Stroman
Uandruantz Ferrell (infant & teen)
Vioris Ferrell
Xenia Brown

Other Cornrows & Co. Publications

Where Beauty Touches Me: Natural Hair Care and Beauty Book

*Let's Talk Hair: Every Black Woman's Personal
Consultation for Healthy Growing Hair"*

Braid Care Instruction Booklet

Thunderhead Hair Care Video for Moms & Dads

Cornrows & Co.
Natural Hair Care Products

Shampoos, Conditioners, Hair Oils, Scalp Tonics and more

To receive a free product brochure call:
Toll free 1(800) 543-3448 ▪ Local calls (202) 723-1827

Write to me and tell me how you feel about your hair.
Cornrows & Co.
5401 14th Street NW
Washington, DC 20011

E-mail — talknhair@aol.com

Reference Books

The Bantam Medical Dictionary. New York: Bantam Books, 1994

Ferrell, Pamela. *Let's Talk Hair*. Washington, DC: Cornrows & Co. Publications, 1997.

Murray, Michael T., N.D. *Encyclopedia of Nutritional Supplements*. Rockland, CA: Prima Publishing, 1996.

Tenney, Louise. *Today's Herbal Health*. Provo, Utah: Woodland Books, 2nd ed., 1983.

Credits & Acknowledgments

Hair by:

Corene Lathern, Felicita Villatoro, Roberta Green, Sade Ojo, Sharon Lyons, Shuletta Moore, Tamara Williams, Tonya Mitchell, Victoria Kioko

Children's clothing designed by:

Anne Hemphill of Amadi's Place, Washington, DC (202) 526-4573
Niambi Davis of Ayana-Nana, Centreville, MD (410) 758-8649

Master Barber advice:

James Spruill of Spruill Barbershop, Washington, DC

Computer technical and graphic support:

Andre Richardson

Personal assistant services:

Juan Laster of Minding Your Business, Inc., Washington DC,

Editorial service:

I want to thank my editor Sabrina Holcomb, for her great ideas and long evenings of editorial support.

Children's Defense Fund, Washington DC

Thanks to an organization that "Stands for Children." CDF is a private non-profit organization providing a voice for the children of America who cannot vote, lobby or speak for themselves. Get more information by visiting their website at: www.childrensdefense.org

INDEX

The Author

I'm **Pamela Ferrell**, a.k.a. Auntie, the author of this book. I have a natural hair care salon where I braid, style hair and write books. I also travel around the country talking about the importance of taking good care of your hair. In my spare time I make videos, play with my bird Rabe and ride my scooter board.

Grown-ups, you might be interested to know that Ferrell is a natural hair care pioneer and political activist who has worked to preserve the cultural practice of hairbraiding in America. She is a member of the DC Barber & Cosmetology Board and the American Hairbraiders & Natural Hair care Association. She is also a registered Doctor of Naturopathy. Co-owner of Cornrows & Co. natural hair care salon, Ferrell is known for her beautiful signature hair designs. She served as hair designer for the film *Daughters of the Dust* and hair stylist to Diana Ross, former Senator Carol Moseley Braun and other notable women. Author of three other natural hair care braid books, she has also produced the *Thunderhead* natural hair care video for parents and kids.